AI VS HUMAN

RAKESH SINGH

ISBN: 978-93-5679-399-6

DEDICATION

To All Human Beings

To those who work silently.
To those who feel tired but keep going.
To those who are expected to perform like machines but still feel deeply.

This book is for you

Table of Contents

INTRODUCTION

When the Screen Lights Up Before the Sun

We wake up to alarms set by machines.
We talk to devices before we talk to people.
We measure productivity in numbers, not in well-being.

From switching on lights to switching off emotions at work, technology now walks with us every moment of our day. Artificial Intelligence has made life easier, faster, and smarter—but somewhere along the way, humans have started feeling replaceable.

This book is not a protest against AI.
It is a reminder—to ourselves and to the world—that **humans are not machines**.

AI can learn patterns.
AI can process data.
AI can replace tasks.

But AI cannot feel exhaustion after giving its best.
AI cannot feel joy after helping someone.
AI cannot feel pain, love, fear, hope, or purpose.

This book is about **balance**.
About using technology wisely without letting it use us.
About preserving emotions in a world obsessed with efficiency.
About choosing humanity—every single day.

PREFACE

Before the Machine Learns How to Feel

Every morning, before we even open our eyes, technology is already awake.

An alarm rings.
A notification blinks.
A screen demands attention.

We scroll before we breathe.
We respond before we feel.
We rush—without asking where we are going.

Somewhere between faster internet and smarter machines, humans have started feeling **slower, tired, and replaceable**.

This book is not written to fight technology.
It is written to **protect humanity**.

AI is powerful.
Technology is necessary.
Progress is inevitable.

But exhaustion should not be the price of progress.
Loss of emotions should not be the cost of efficiency.
Humans should not be treated like machines.

A machine can work 24×7—but even a machine needs rest, oiling, and maintenance.
A human gives emotions, effort, creativity, patience, and soul—yet is expected to perform endlessly.

This book asks one simple question:

If machines are treated better than humans…
what exactly are we becoming?

These pages are for professionals who feel burnt out.
For employees who feel invisible.
For leaders who want to lead with empathy.
For parents raising children in a digital world.
For anyone who feels that technology is advancing—but humanity is lagging behind.

We don't need to reject AI.
We need to **remember who we are**.

Because no algorithm can replace empathy.
No data can replicate love.
No machine can feel what it means to be human.

Chapter 1: The Day Technology Took Over Without Us Noticing

No one remembers the exact day it happened.

There was no announcement.
No warning.
No moment when we said, *"From today, life will change."*

It just… did.

One day, you switched off the light using a switch.
Another day, you asked a device to do it for you.

One day, you waited for someone to come home to talk.
Another day, you sent a message and expected an instant reply.

One day, you thought deeply before making decisions.
Another day, you trusted an app to decide for you.

Technology didn't knock on the door.
It quietly walked in—and we moved aside because it felt helpful.

At first, it was a blessing.

Life became easier.
Faster.
More comfortable.

Why walk when you can order?
Why remember when you can search?
Why wait when you can automate?

Slowly, comfort turned into habit.
Habit turned into dependency.
Dependency turned into routine.

And routine turned into **life**.

We didn't choose this speed.
We adapted to it.

When Convenience Became Control

Technology promised us time.

But somewhere along the way, it started taking it back—piece by piece.

We save time on travel, yet we are always busy.
We save time on work, yet we never log off mentally.
We save time on communication, yet conversations feel shallow.

Our phones are always with us.
On the bed.

On the table.
In our pockets.
In our hands.

Sometimes, even in our dreams.

We don't wait anymore.
Waiting feels uncomfortable now.

A slow internet connection irritates us.
A delayed reply makes us anxious.
A pause in response feels like rejection.

Technology trained us—not by force, but by **reward**.

Instant results.
Instant likes.
Instant replies.
Instant validation.

And slowly, our patience disappeared.

Homes That Became Smarter, Humans Who Became Tired

Our homes learned our habits.

Lights turn on automatically.
Doors unlock remotely.
Cameras watch silently.

Machines understand our schedules better than people do.

But while homes became smarter, humans became more exhausted.

We wake up with alarms.
We sleep with screens.
Even silence is filled with notifications.

We sit together, yet everyone looks at their own device.
Families share rooms—but not moments.

A child learns to swipe before learning to write.
A parent scrolls while the child speaks.

No one is bad here.
No one is careless.

We are just **busy surviving in a fast world**.

Offices That Never Close

Work used to have boundaries.

There was a time when leaving the office meant leaving work behind.

Now, work travels with us.

In our phones.
In our emails.
In our thoughts.

A message at night.
A call on weekends.
A task "just five minutes" before sleep.

Technology made work flexible—but also **endless**.

The body goes home.
The mind stays logged in.

Employees are available, but not present.
Efficient, but emotionally drained.

Performance is measured.
Feelings are not.

No one asks, *"Are you tired?"*
They ask, *"Is the task done?"*

Relationships in the Age of Screens

We are more connected than ever.

Yet loneliness is everywhere.

We send emojis instead of expressions.
We type feelings instead of saying them.
We read messages without hearing the tone.

Misunderstandings grow faster than understanding.

We see everyone's happy moments online.
We hide our tired ones offline.

Comparison becomes natural.
Contentment becomes rare.

Technology didn't destroy relationships.
But it **changed how we show up in them**.

Presence became optional.
Attention became divided.

When Thinking Was Outsourced

Earlier, we used to remember phone numbers.
Now we remember passwords—and still forget them.

Earlier, we planned routes.
Now we follow maps.

Earlier, we debated choices.
Now we trust recommendations.

What to watch.
What to buy.
Where to go.
What to read.

Algorithms know us well.

Sometimes better than we know ourselves.

This is not wrong.
This is powerful.

But it comes with a cost.

When machines start thinking for us,
humans stop questioning.

Dependency doesn't arrive loudly.
It arrives politely.

"Let me help you."
"This will save time."
"You'll love this."

And we agree—because it feels good.

We Adapted, Not Chose

This is the most important truth.

We didn't wake up one day and say,
"I want life to be this fast."
"I want to feel this tired."
"I want to be always reachable."

We adapted because everyone else did.

We adapted to survive.
We adapted to compete.
We adapted to stay relevant.

Speed became normal.
Overload became normal.
Exhaustion became normal.

And when something is normal, we stop questioning it.

The Shape of Our Habits

Automation changes habits quietly.

When everything is automated:

- We expect less effort
- We tolerate less delay

- We feel frustrated faster

Small inconveniences feel unbearable.

Waiting feels like wasting time.
Silence feels uncomfortable.
Doing nothing feels unproductive.

Even rest needs justification now.

"I'm resting to be productive."
"I'm taking a break to work better."

We forgot how to rest just to be human.

This Chapter Is Not a Warning—It Is Awareness

Technology is not the enemy.

AI is not the villain.

This book does not ask you to disconnect, resign, or reject progress.

It asks something simpler—and more powerful.

To notice.

To notice how deeply technology has entered our lives.
To notice how habits have changed.
To notice how thinking has shifted.
To notice how tired we feel—and why.

Awareness is the first step toward balance.

Because once you see the speed,
you can choose when to slow down.

Once you see dependency,
you can decide where to pause.

Once you see the machine around you,
you can protect the human within you.

A Quiet Question to End This Chapter

If technology stopped for one day…

Would you feel free?
Or anxious?

The answer matters.

Because this book is not about machines.

It is about **us**.

And this is just the beginning.

Chapter 2: Convenience vs Consciousness

Convenience feels like kindness.

It tells us, *"Relax. I've got this."*
It removes effort.
It saves time.
It makes life smoother.

And that is why we love it.

But convenience has a silent twin—unawareness.

Not because convenience is bad,
but because when life becomes too easy,
we stop paying attention.

The Comfort That Puts Us to Sleep

Think about your daily routine.

You wake up with an alarm.
You check your phone before your thoughts.
You scroll while brushing.

You scroll while eating.
You scroll while resting.

None of this feels harmful.

It feels normal.

That is the danger—not pain, but comfort.

When something doesn't hurt,
we don't question it.

Convenience slowly trains us to live on autopilot.

We don't ask:

- Why am I doing this?
- Do I really need this?
- Is this helping me—or replacing me?

We just accept.

When Choice Disappears Quietly

Earlier, choices required effort.

What to cook.
What to read.
What to watch.
What to buy.

Now, everything is suggested.

"Recommended for you."
"People like you also bought."
"You may enjoy this."

It feels helpful.
It feels personal.

But over time, suggestions become decisions.

We don't explore—we select.
We don't search—we follow.

Convenience removes friction,
but friction is where thinking lives.

When everything flows easily,
thinking becomes optional.

The Cost We Don't See

Convenience saves time,
but it slowly steals **awareness**.

We eat faster, but enjoy less.
We travel easier, but notice less.
We work faster, but feel emptier.

We finish tasks,
but forget ourselves.

This is not laziness.
This is conditioning.

The brain loves ease.
The brain avoids effort.

Technology feeds the brain exactly what it wants.

And slowly, we forget how to pause.

Consciousness Is Effort

Being conscious requires energy.

To stop scrolling.
To feel boredom.
To sit with silence.
To think deeply.

Convenience avoids all of that.

Why feel boredom when there is content?
Why think when there is an answer?
Why wait when there is speed?

But boredom is where creativity is born.
Silence is where emotions speak.
Effort is where meaning lives.

Convenience removes pain—but also removes depth.

Living Without Feeling Present

Have you ever reached a place and not remembered the journey?

Have you ever finished a meal without tasting it?

Have you ever completed a day without remembering anything meaningful?

That is life on autopilot.

We are present physically,
but absent emotionally.

We respond faster,
but feel slower.

Convenience trains us to move—but not to feel.

When Ease Becomes Expectation

Once convenience enters life,
we expect it everywhere.

We expect instant service.
Instant replies.
Instant results.

And when we don't get them,
we feel frustrated—not because it's wrong,
but because our tolerance has reduced.

Waiting feels like injustice.
Delays feel like disrespect.

Our patience didn't shrink by accident.

It was replaced.

The Workplace Example We Ignore

Automation makes work efficient.

Reports generated automatically.
Decisions guided by data.
Performance measured instantly.

This is powerful.

But when work becomes too optimized,
humans are treated like extensions of systems.

Output matters.
Presence doesn't.

Fatigue is invisible.
Burnout is silent.

Even machines need maintenance.
Humans are expected to run endlessly.

Convenience at work improves numbers,
but consciousness protects people.

Awareness Is Not Rejection

This book is not asking you to reject convenience.

It is asking you to balance it.

Use technology,
but don't let it use you.

Let machines handle tasks,
but let humans handle meaning.

Convenience should support life—
not replace experience.

Small Acts of Conscious Living

Consciousness doesn't require big changes.

It begins quietly.

Eating without a screen.
Walking without headphones.
Thinking before tapping "accept."
Asking, *"Do I need this?"*

These are small pauses.

But pauses are powerful.

They bring you back to yourself.

A Gentle Truth

Convenience makes life easier.
Consciousness makes life worth living.

Without consciousness,
we may live longer—but emptier.

Without awareness,
we may function better—but feel less.

Technology can run our lives,
but only **we** can live them.

A Question to Carry Forward

The next time something becomes easier, ask yourself:

Is this helping me live better…
or helping me live less consciously?

That question changes everything.

Chapter 3: From Employees to Resources

Technology made life comfortable.
But somewhere along the way, it also changed how we are **seen**.

Not as people.
Not as humans with limits.
But as **resources**.

When Work Stopped Feeling Human

There was a time when work had rhythm.

You arrived.
You spoke to people.
You worked.
You left.

Now, work follows you home.

Emails at night.
Messages on weekends.
Calls during dinner.
Notifications before sleep.

Technology didn't knock.
It walked in silently.

And because it helped us work better,
we let it stay.

Efficiency Became the New Emotion

Earlier, effort mattered.

Now, output matters.

Earlier, dedication was visible.

Now, availability is expected.

The question is no longer:
"How are you managing?"

It is:
"Why wasn't this done faster?"

Technology gave speed.
Workplaces took it as a promise.

And slowly, speed became the standard.

We Saved Time… But Lost Ourselves

Everything is faster now.

Reports are auto-generated.
Meetings are virtual.
Decisions are data-driven.

We should have more time.

But we don't.

We are always rushing.
Always catching up.
Always behind.

Time was saved—
but peace was not.

Because time saved was not returned to humans.
It was given back to work.

The Silent Shift in Language

Notice the words we use now.

"Resource allocation."
"Human capital."
"Utilization rate."
"Productivity metrics."

These words are not wrong.

But they are cold.

They measure performance—
not presence.

They track numbers—
not emotions.

A human being slowly became a data point.

When Attention Became a Scarce Resource

Technology demands attention constantly.

Alerts.
Updates.
Dashboards.
Deadlines.

Your focus is always split.

Even while working,
your mind is juggling multiple tasks.

This is called multitasking.

But the human brain doesn't multitask.
It **switches rapidly**.

And switching drains energy.

We finish the day exhausted—
without doing heavy work.

Not because we worked too much,
but because our attention was never whole.

Patience Is No Longer Valued

Earlier, learning took time.

Now, everything is urgent.

Training is rushed.
Growth is expected instantly.
Mistakes are costly.

Technology reduced waiting time—
but also reduced tolerance.

There is no space to be slow.
No space to struggle.
No space to learn gradually.

And yet, humans are not software updates.

Presence Is the First Casualty

Being present is difficult now.

At work, we think about deadlines.
At home, we think about work.
During rest, we think about messages.

We are everywhere—
except where we are.

Technology didn't steal presence.

We traded it for convenience.

The Emotional Cost We Ignore

Burnout doesn't arrive suddenly.

It comes quietly.

Through tired eyes.
Through short tempers.
Through constant fatigue.
Through loss of motivation.

People don't quit jobs anymore.

They quit **pressure without empathy**.

They quit being treated like machines.

Even Machines Get Maintenance

Machines need servicing.
Machines need upgrades.
Machines need downtime.

But humans?

Expected to perform.
Expected to adapt.
Expected to stay available.

No rest.
No pause.
No slowing down.

This is not progress.

This is imbalance.

Mindfulness Is Not Slowness

Mindfulness does not mean working less.

It means working humanly.

It means:

- Space to think
- Permission to rest
- Time to recover
- Respect for limits

Technology can support this.

But only if we choose consciousness over control.

A Workplace Can Be Smart and Kind

Efficiency and empathy are not enemies.

Technology should assist humans—
not replace their value.

Data should guide decisions—
not erase emotions.

When workplaces remember this,
people don't just perform.

They belong.

A Quiet Truth

We saved time.
But lost patience.

We gained speed.
But lost presence.

We became efficient.
But less mindful.

Technology didn't do this alone.

We allowed it—
without asking what it was taking in return.

A Question to Carry Forward

The next time work demands more speed, ask:

Are we optimizing systems…
or exhausting people?

The answer decides the future.

Chapter 4: Even Machines Need Rest—Why Don't Humans Get Any?

A machine breaks down if it is overused.

A human being is expected to continue.

Machines Are Respected. Humans Are Tested.

Every machine comes with a manual.

It clearly says:

- How long it can run
- When it needs rest
- When it needs servicing
- What happens if you ignore warnings

When a machine shows signs of stress,
we don't shout at it.

We stop it.
We repair it.
We give it time.

But when a human shows the same signs—
fatigue, slow response, emotional exhaustion—
we say:

"Be stronger."
"Adjust."
"This is normal."
"Everyone is doing it."

Machines are protected.
Humans are pressured.

The Body Gives Warnings. We Ignore Them.

A machine overheats.
A human burns out.

But burnout doesn't smoke.
It doesn't make noise.

It hides.

Behind forced smiles.
Behind late nights.
Behind silent tears.
Behind the phrase: *"I'm fine."*

The body whispers first.

Then it screams.

Most of us listen only when it breaks.

Sleep Is Not Laziness. It Is Repair.

When a phone battery drops to 5%,
we panic.

When our own energy drops to zero,
we continue.

Sleep is not rest alone.

It is:

- Memory repair
- Emotional balance
- Hormonal reset
- Mental clarity

Without sleep, the brain suffers.
Decision-making weakens.
Emotions overflow.
Focus collapses.

Still, people proudly say:
"I slept only four hours."

As if exhaustion is an achievement.

Nutrition Is Fuel, Not Decoration.

A machine needs the right fuel.

Low quality fuel damages it.

Humans know this.

Yet we skip meals.
Eat in rush.
Eat stress.
Drink caffeine instead of rest.

We treat our bodies like temporary tools—
forgetting we must live in them forever.

Emotional Recovery Is Real.

Machines don't feel.

Humans do.

And emotions also need recovery.

Unspoken pain accumulates.
Unexpressed stress settles in the body.
Unacknowledged fear turns into anxiety.

Rest is not only physical.

It is:

- Silence

- Being heard
- Feeling safe
- Feeling valued

Without emotional rest,
even sleep doesn't heal.

Workplaces Forget One Simple Truth

A tired human makes mistakes.

A burnt-out human loses creativity.

A neglected human stops caring.

Machines produce.
Humans **create**.

Creation needs rest.

Why We Feel Guilty for Resting

Somewhere along the way,
rest became shameful.

If you rest, you are weak.
If you pause, you are lazy.
If you say no, you are difficult.

So people rest secretly.
Sleep late secretly.
Cry silently.

Machines don't feel guilty when they shut down.

Humans do.

Science Has Already Warned Us

Lack of rest causes:

- Reduced immunity
- Memory loss
- Emotional instability
- Heart disease
- Depression

This is not emotion.

This is evidence.

But culture often ignores science
when productivity is involved.

Humans Are Not Renewable Energy

You cannot drain a human endlessly
and expect infinite output.

Rest restores.
Sleep repairs.
Nutrition fuels.
Emotional safety heals.

Without these, humans don't grow.

They survive.

A Gentle Reframe

Rest is not stopping.

Rest is preparing.

Rest is not weakness.

Rest is wisdom.

If we want sustainable progress,
we must protect humans
the way we protect machines.

The Question That Matters

If we care so deeply about machines breaking down…

Why do we wait for humans to collapse
before caring?

A Quiet Promise

The future does not need faster humans.

It needs healthier ones.

And health begins with permission to rest.

Chapter 5: Emotional Intelligence vs Artificial Intelligence

Artificial Intelligence is learning fast.

But there is something it will never learn.

How it feels to be human.

What AI Does Exceptionally Well

AI processes data faster than any human ever could.

It remembers everything.
It never gets tired.
It never forgets.
It never doubts itself.

It predicts patterns.
Optimizes systems.
Improves efficiency.

And yes—
it makes life easier.

This is not a threat.

This is progress.

But progress without understanding
can become pressure.

What AI Will Never Feel

AI does not feel fear before a difficult conversation.

AI does not feel joy when someone believes in it.

AI does not feel pain when rejected.

AI does not carry guilt, hope, shame, or love.

It can **recognize** emotions.
It can **label** emotions.
It can **respond** to emotions.

But it cannot **experience** them.

And that difference changes everything.

Emotional Intelligence Is Invisible—but Powerful

Emotional Intelligence lives in moments we don't measure.

In a manager who notices silence.
In a colleague who listens without fixing.
In a leader who chooses kindness over speed.

These moments don't appear in dashboards.

But they build trust.
They build loyalty.
They build meaning.

AI cannot replace that.

The Danger of Confusing Accuracy with Wisdom

AI can be right.

But being right is not the same as being wise.

Wisdom knows:

- When to pause
- When to soften words
- When to choose people over process

AI does not understand context like humans do.

It calculates outcomes.
Humans feel consequences.

Human Judgment Is Emotional—and That's Not a Flaw

We often hear:
"Emotions should be removed from decisions."

But emotions are not weakness.

They are information.

Empathy warns us.
Fear protects us.
Compassion connects us.

Removing emotion creates cold systems.

Cold systems break humans.

Why People Fear Being Replaced

The fear is not about technology.

It is about being **devalued**.

When speed matters more than care,
when output matters more than effort,
when availability matters more than wellbeing—

People start to feel invisible.

Not replaced.

But forgotten.

AI Should Assist, Not Author Life

AI can recommend.

Humans must decide.

AI can analyze.

Humans must understand.

AI can automate.

Humans must empathize.

The healthiest future is not AI vs Humans.

It is AI **with** Humans.

Where Humans Will Always Lead

In care.
In creativity.
In compassion.
In ethics.
In meaning.

Machines execute tasks.

Humans carry responsibility.

A Workplace Without Emotional Intelligence Is Dangerous

A system without empathy becomes efficient—and cruel.

People follow rules.
But stop caring.

They perform.
But don't belong.

This is how burnout spreads quietly.

The Truth We Need to Accept

AI is powerful.

But power without emotional intelligence
needs human guidance.

We don't need smarter machines alone.

We need **wiser humans**.

The Choice Before Us

Will we build systems that understand data
but ignore hearts?

Or systems that use intelligence
without losing humanity?

The future is watching what we choose.

A Final Thought

Artificial Intelligence can improve life.

Emotional Intelligence gives it meaning.

One optimizes the world.

The other saves it.

Chapter 6: AI Can Replace Skills, Not Souls

The fear is real.

It sits quietly in the back of the mind.

"What if I become unnecessary?"

The Fear Nobody Wants to Admit

People don't fear AI because it is intelligent.

They fear it because it is fast, tireless, and improving every day.

They fear waking up one morning
and realizing that something they spent years learning
can now be done by a machine in seconds.

This fear is human.

And it deserves honesty—not denial.

Skills Have Always Changed

Once, typing was a skill.

Once, calculating by hand was a skill.

Once, memorizing information was power.

Technology didn't end humans then.

It shifted **what mattered**.

Skills evolve.

Souls don't.

What AI Can Replace

AI can replace:

- Repetitive tasks
- Pattern recognition
- Data analysis
- Speed-based execution

AI is brilliant at consistency.

It does not get bored.

It does not lose focus.

It does not complain.

And that is exactly why it exists.

To take away what drains humans.

What AI Will Never Replace

AI will never feel responsibility.

It will never feel guilt when it hurts someone.

It will never feel pride when a person grows.

It will never carry regret.

It does not know what it means to try and fail.

It does not know what it means to care.

A Soul Is Not a Function

A soul is not productivity.

A soul is not output.

A soul is:

- Empathy

- Values
- Judgment
- Meaning
- Conscience

AI can simulate understanding.

Humans live it.

Confidence Comes from Knowing Your Depth

Fear comes from comparing speed.

Confidence comes from knowing depth.

Machines go wide.

Humans go deep.

AI can answer questions.

Humans ask *why they matter*.

The Human Qualities That Will Always Matter

In any future—no matter how advanced—these will remain human strengths:

- Emotional connection
- Moral decision-making
- Creativity born from pain and joy

- Leadership through trust
- Healing through presence

These are not downloadable.

Why Fear Shrinks When Purpose Grows

People who feel replaceable
often feel unseen.

Not because they lack value—
but because their value was never named.

The moment you understand your human role,
fear loses its grip.

The Future Needs Humans More Than Ever

As technology grows smarter,
humans must grow wiser.

Someone must:

- Decide what is ethical
- Protect what is humane
- Balance progress with compassion

That responsibility belongs to humans.

We Are Not Competing with AI

We are partnering with it.

AI handles efficiency.

Humans handle meaning.

AI processes information.

Humans process life.

A Quiet Truth to Hold Onto

If you feel afraid, it means you care.

If you care, you are still human.

And as long as humanity exists,
souls will never be replaced.

A Reassuring Ending

AI may replace skills.

But it will never replace
your ability to feel, to care, to choose, and to love.

And those are not weaknesses.

They are the reason the future still needs humans.

When People Start Measuring Themselves Like Machines

One of the biggest mistakes we are making today
is comparing humans to machines
using machine standards.

Speed.
Accuracy.
Availability.
Output.

When humans are measured this way,
they will always feel insufficient.

Because humans were never designed to win on speed alone.

A machine can work all night.
A human needs sleep.

A machine can repeat endlessly.
A human needs meaning.

And that difference is not a flaw.
It is the design.

The Pressure to Become "More Machine-Like"

People are silently changing themselves to survive.

They suppress emotions at work.
They hide exhaustion.

They stop asking questions.
They stop showing vulnerability.

They try to act efficient instead of authentic.

But the more human qualities we hide,
the more replaceable we actually become.

Because when humans stop being human,
machines truly win.

What Makes a Human Truly Irreplaceable

It is not knowledge alone.

Knowledge can be stored.

It is not skill alone.

Skills can be automated.

What cannot be replaced is **context**.

A human understands:

- When silence means pain
- When anger is actually fear
- When productivity is hiding burnout
- When rules need flexibility

AI sees data.

Humans see people.

Mistakes Are Not Human Weaknesses—They Are Human Proof

Machines avoid mistakes.

Humans learn from them.

Every failure carries emotion:
disappointment, reflection, growth.

AI does not grow from failure.

It is corrected.

Humans grow *through* failure.

That growth changes judgment, empathy, and wisdom.

And wisdom cannot be programmed.

The Future Belongs to Those Who Stay Human

The safest place in the future
is not in being the fastest worker.

It is in being the most *aware* one.

Aware of:

- People
- Ethics
- Impact

- Responsibility

The world will need humans
who can slow things down when speed becomes dangerous.

Leadership Will Never Be Automated

AI can manage schedules.

It cannot inspire trust.

AI can suggest decisions.

It cannot stand with someone during uncertainty.

Leadership is not command.

Leadership is presence.

And presence is deeply human.

Why Confidence Matters More Than Skill Now

Skills will change again and again.

Confidence rooted in humanity does not.

When people understand this,
they stop chasing relevance through exhaustion.

They start building relevance through depth.

A Gentle Reminder for the Reader

You are not behind.

You are not outdated.

You are not weak because you feel tired, anxious, or uncertain.

You are human.

And humanity is not becoming obsolete.

It is becoming **essential**.

The Real Question Is Not About AI

The real question is:

Will we design a future that remembers
why humans mattered in the first place?

Because machines will do what they are told.

Humans must decide what should be done.

A Quiet Ending to Carry Forward

Skills can be learned.
Skills can be replaced.

But a soul—
with conscience, compassion, and courage—
remains beyond automation.

And as long as that exists,
humans will always have a place in the future.

Chapter 7: The Cost of Progress No One Talks About

Progress looks beautiful from a distance.

Shiny devices.
Faster systems.
Smarter machines.
Bigger promises.

But costs are rarely shown on the cover.

They are hidden in everyday lives.

What Progress Gave Us—and What It Took Away

Progress gave us speed.

But it took away patience.

Progress gave us connectivity.

But it quietly weakened connection.

Progress gave us comfort.

But made discomfort unbearable.

We gained convenience—but lost tolerance for effort.

We Are Always On, But Rarely Present

People wake up to screens.

Work through screens.

Rest with screens.

Even relationships now live through notifications.

We talk more—but listen less.

We respond quickly—but feel slowly.

The body is present.

The mind is scattered.

And the heart feels left behind.

Mental Health Became the Silent Bill

Progress never warned us about this cost.

Anxiety from constant comparison.
Stress from endless availability.
Burnout from no clear ending to workdays.
Loneliness despite being "connected" all the time.

People are not breaking because they are weak.

They are breaking because the pace is inhuman.

We Are Producing More, Feeling Less

Work has become measurable.

Emotions have not.

So emotions are ignored.

People learn to suppress feelings to stay relevant.

They smile in meetings.
Collapse in private.
Scroll endlessly at night.

Progress taught us how to perform.

Not how to cope.

Children Are Growing Up Faster—but Not Deeper

Children learn technology early.

But emotional maturity takes time.

Attention spans shrink.

Silence feels uncomfortable.

Boredom—which once created imagination—is avoided.

We are raising efficient minds
without giving them space to feel.

Relationships Are Efficient—but Fragile

We text instead of talk.

We multitask while listening.

We reply—but don't reflect.

Conflicts are avoided, not resolved.

Technology didn't break relationships.

But it made escaping them easier.

The Pressure to Keep Up

Progress does not pause.

So people don't pause.

Everyone is racing—without knowing where.

Fear of falling behind keeps people exhausted.

Not everyone wants more.

But everyone feels forced to chase it.

Success Without Satisfaction

People achieve milestones.

Good jobs.
Smart homes.
Stable income.

Yet something feels missing.

Because progress focused on *what we can do*—
not *how we feel while doing it*.

We Normalized Exhaustion

Being tired became normal.

Being stressed became common.

Being disconnected became acceptable.

If everyone is struggling,
we stop calling it a problem.

But widespread pain is still pain.

What We Rarely Ask

We ask:
"How fast can we go?"

But we don't ask:
"Should we?"

We ask:
"What's next?"

But not:
"What's enough?"

Progress Needs a Human Pause

Progress is not the enemy.

Blind progress is.

Progress without empathy
turns people into systems.

Progress without rest
turns life into survival.

The Real Cost

The cost of progress is not money.

It is:

- Peace
- Presence
- Patience
- Emotional safety

These losses don't show on charts.

But they shape lives.

A Gentle Truth

Progress should improve life.

Not replace it.

Technology should support humans.

Not demand sacrifices from them.

A Question Worth Carrying

If progress costs us our health, relationships, and humanity—

Is it still progress?

Or just movement without meaning?

The future doesn't need to be slower.

It needs to be **wiser**.

And wisdom begins
when we finally talk about the cost.

Surrounded by Technology, Starved of Connection

We have never been this connected.

And we have never felt this alone.

Messages arrive instantly.
Faces appear on screens.
Voices travel across continents.

Yet, many people sit in crowded rooms
and feel invisible.

Technology filled the space between people—
but emptied the space **within** them.

Loneliness Is Not About Being Alone Anymore

Loneliness today does not mean no company.

It means no **connection**.

You can sit with family
and still feel unheard.

You can work in a team
and still feel unsupported.

You can talk all day
and still feel unseen.

Loneliness now wears busy clothes.

Mental Health Became a Private Struggle

In the digital age, suffering is quiet.

People don’t break loudly.

They scroll.
They smile.
They reply “I’m fine.”

Mental health issues hide behind productivity.

If you are working, you are assumed okay.

No one asks:
“How are you really holding up?”

The Pressure to Perform Never Sleeps

Technology removed boundaries.

Work follows us home.

Rest feels guilty.

Silence feels unproductive.

People are always "on."

And being always on
means never fully resting.

Emotional Disconnect at Work

People are evaluated by output.

Not by effort.
Not by stress.
Not by emotional load.

A person may be carrying:

- Fear of job loss
- Family responsibilities
- Health struggles
- Emotional fatigue

But systems don't ask.

They only measure results.

Invisible Suffering Becomes Normalized

When everyone is tired,
tiredness becomes normal.

When everyone is stressed,
stress becomes expected.

When everyone is anxious,
anxiety becomes invisible.

We stop noticing pain
because it is everywhere.

Social Media: Together but Apart

Social platforms show lives—
not realities.

People compare:

- Highlights with struggles
- Success with self-doubt
- Perfection with exhaustion

This constant comparison
creates quiet self-blame.

People think:
"Everyone is managing. Why can't I?"

Emotional Debt Is Real

Every ignored emotion accumulates.

Every suppressed feeling adds weight.

Every unexpressed fear becomes pressure.

This is emotional debt.

And like financial debt,
it grows quietly—until it demands payment.

Payment comes as:

- Burnout
- Depression
- Anxiety
- Emotional numbness

Why People Don't Speak

Because vulnerability feels risky.

Because speed is valued over honesty.

Because emotions slow things down.

Because people fear being seen as weak.

So they suffer quietly.

Technology Didn’t Create This—But It Accelerated It

Technology didn’t remove empathy.

But it made it optional.

Technology didn’t remove care.

But it made avoidance easier.

And when care becomes optional,
many choose convenience.

What Healing Begins With

Not rejection of technology.

But recognition of humanity.

It begins when:

- Listening becomes intentional
- Rest becomes respected
- Boundaries become normal
- Emotions become valid

A Gentle Wake-Up Call

Humans are not designed
for constant performance.

We are designed for rhythm.

Work.
Rest.
Connection.
Meaning.

When one is missing,
everything suffers.

A Quiet Truth to Sit With

Being surrounded by technology
should not mean living emotionally alone.

Progress should not require silence.

And no one should have to suffer invisibly
to be considered successful.

Closing Thought for This Chapter

The cost of progress is not visible on screens.

It is felt in hearts.

And until we acknowledge that cost,
we will keep moving forward
while slowly breaking inside.

Chapter 8: Living With AI, Not Competing Against It

We were never meant to race against machines.

We were meant to **use them**.

The Wrong Question We Keep Asking

Most conversations start with fear:

"Will AI take my job?"
"Will humans become useless?"
"Will machines replace us?"

These questions come from comparison.

And comparison creates anxiety.

The better question is:

How can AI support human life instead of replacing it?

AI Is a Tool, Not an Opponent

A hammer didn't replace the carpenter.

A calculator didn't replace the mathematician.

Technology has always extended human ability.

AI is no different.

It removes friction.
It handles repetition.
It increases accuracy.

But it does not create meaning.

Competition Makes Humans Lose

When humans try to compete with AI on speed or efficiency, they exhaust themselves.

Because machines were built for those things.

Humans were built for:

- Understanding
- Adaptability
- Emotional awareness
- Ethical judgment

Trying to be machine-like
makes humans less human.

And more replaceable.

The Real Skill Is Collaboration

The future belongs to people who know:

- What to delegate to AI
- What to keep human
- When to trust data
- When to trust intuition

AI handles information.

Humans handle interpretation.

Work Becomes Healthier When Roles Are Clear

When AI handles:

- Repetitive tasks
- Data-heavy analysis
- Scheduling and automation

Humans get space for:

- Creativity
- Problem-solving
- Relationship-building
- Strategic thinking

This is not loss.

This is liberation.

Fear Reduces When Understanding Increases

Fear often comes from uncertainty.

When people understand how AI works,
they stop fearing it.

They see it as support.

Not replacement.

Learning to Work With AI Is a Human Skill

Curiosity beats resistance.

Learning how to use AI
keeps humans relevant and confident.

Not by becoming technical experts—
but by becoming wise users.

Where Humans Must Stay in Control

AI should advise.

Humans must decide.

AI should suggest.

Humans must judge.

AI should support.

Humans must lead.

Without human oversight,
technology becomes directionless.

The Human Touch Still Matters

A customer remembers how they were treated.

An employee remembers how they were respected.

A patient remembers how they were comforted.

AI cannot replicate care.

Redefining Success in the AI Age

Success is not speed alone.

It is:

- Balance
- Sustainability
- Wellbeing
- Purpose

AI can help reach success.

But humans must define it.

A Gentle Reminder

You don’t need to outrun machines.

You need to **out-human** them.

The Peaceful Ending

When humans stop competing with AI
and start cooperating with it,

Fear fades.
Confidence grows.
Work becomes meaningful again.

The future does not belong to machines.

It belongs to humans
who know how to use them wisely.

Chapter 9: The Emotion Economy

For a long time, emotions were treated like distractions.

Something to manage.
Something to hide.
Something to control.

But the future is quietly proving something else:

Feelings are not weaknesses.
They are power.

Why the Old Definition of Value Is Fading

The industrial age rewarded:

- Speed
- Obedience
- Output

The digital age rewarded:

- Knowledge
- Accuracy
- Efficiency

The future will reward:

- Empathy
- Ethics
- Creativity
- Emotional intelligence

Because machines now do the first two better than humans ever could.

What remains is what only humans can offer.

What the Emotion Economy Really Means

The emotion economy is not about being emotional.

It is about being **aware**.

Aware of:

- How decisions affect people
- How pressure impacts wellbeing
- How culture shapes performance
- How trust fuels productivity

In the emotion economy, success is measured not just by profit—but by **people**.

Empathy Is the New Leadership Skill

People don't leave companies.

They leave environments.

They leave when:

- They feel unheard
- They feel unsafe
- They feel invisible

Empathy creates belonging.

Belonging creates loyalty.

Loyalty creates sustainable success.

Ethics Will Matter More Than Innovation

Just because something can be built
does not mean it should be used blindly.

Ethical judgment will define the future.

Humans must decide:

- Where AI is appropriate
- Where privacy is sacred
- Where efficiency should stop

Technology needs conscience.

Only humans provide that.

Creativity Cannot Be Automated

AI can generate.

Humans create.

Creation comes from:

- Experience
- Pain
- Joy
- Curiosity

Creativity connects logic with emotion.

And connection is what people remember.

Emotional Intelligence Builds Strong Systems

Emotionally intelligent organizations:

- Communicate better
- Handle conflict faster
- Recover from failure stronger
- Retain talent longer

They don’t ignore performance.

They humanize it.

Why Society Must Invest in Emotional Skills

Education teaches facts.

Life demands feelings.

Without emotional intelligence:

- Conflict increases
- Burnout spreads
- Trust erodes

Societies that value emotional literacy create healthier citizens.

The Economic Value of Being Human

Happy people work better.

Heard people innovate more.

Respected people stay longer.

This is not idealism.

It is reality.

Feelings Drive Decisions

Every purchase.
Every partnership.
Every commitment.

People decide emotionally—
then justify logically.

Ignoring emotion
means misunderstanding behavior.

The Quiet Shift Already Happening

The most respected leaders today:

- Listen more
- Speak thoughtfully
- Act responsibly

They are not louder.

They are wiser.

A Message to the Reader

If you are empathetic, sensitive, thoughtful, creative—

You are not behind.

You are prepared.

The Closing Truth

In a world of artificial intelligence,
human intelligence becomes emotional.

And those who feel deeply
will shape the future.

Teaching Emotional Intelligence in a Digital World-

Technology is taught everywhere.

Emotions are taught almost nowhere.

Yet in a world ruled by screens, speed, and systems, **emotional intelligence has become a survival skill**, not a luxury.

This chapter explores why teaching emotional intelligence—at home, in schools, and at workplaces—is no longer optional.

Why Emotional Intelligence Must Be Taught Now

Children learn to use devices before they learn to express feelings.

Employees learn tools before they learn boundaries.

Leaders learn strategy before they learn empathy.

The result:

- Smart minds
- Untrained hearts

Emotional intelligence fills this gap.

What Emotional Intelligence Really Includes

Emotional intelligence is not about being soft.

It is about being **aware and balanced**.

It includes:

- Self-awareness
- Emotional regulation
- Empathy
- Active listening
- Ethical decision-making

These skills protect humans from becoming robotic in a digital world.

Teaching EI to Children in a Screen-First World

Children today grow up connected—but not always understood.

Teaching EI helps them:

- Name their emotions
- Manage frustration
- Build real relationships
- Handle online pressure

Technology should assist learning—not replace emotional growth.

Emotional Intelligence at Workplaces

Companies train employees on:

- Software
- Processes
- Metrics

But ignore:

- Burnout
- Stress
- Human limits

Teaching EI at work improves:

- Collaboration
- Leadership
- Mental health
- Long-term performance

Leaders as Emotional Educators

Leaders teach EI not by lectures—but by behavior.

When leaders:

- Listen
- Respect boundaries
- Admit mistakes

They create emotionally safe cultures.

Balancing Digital Tools with Human Teaching

AI can personalize learning.

Humans must personalize care.

Technology should support:

- Reflection
- Feedback
- Emotional check-ins

Not replace human connection.

The Long-Term Impact

Emotionally intelligent societies:

- Handle conflict better

- Adapt faster
- Stay humane

Teaching EI ensures progress does not erase compassion.

Core Message of the Chapter

If we teach only technology,
we create skilled machines.

If we teach emotional intelligence,
we raise balanced humans.

Closing Thought

The future does not need more efficient people.

It needs **emotionally aware humans who know how to use technology without losing themselves**.

Chapter 10: Choosing Humanity Every Day

The future is not something that will happen to us.

The future is something we are creating—**one choice at a time**.

Every day, we wake up and make small decisions that shape the kind of world we live in.
We choose speed or presence.
Convenience or consciousness.
Performance or purpose.

Humanity is not lost in one dramatic moment.
It fades slowly—when we stop paying attention.

And the truth is this:
The future is still ours—if we choose it.

Humanity Is a Daily Practice, Not a Philosophy

Being human is not automatic anymore.

In a world driven by algorithms, reminders, notifications, and deadlines, humanity requires effort.

It requires pausing when everything pushes us to rush.
It requires listening when everything tells us to respond.
It requires feeling when everything encourages numbness.

Choosing humanity is not about rejecting technology.
It is about **refusing to disappear inside it**.

Setting Boundaries in a Boundaryless World

Technology does not know when to stop.

Humans must.

Emails do not sleep.
Messages do not rest.
Deadlines do not feel guilt.

But you do.

Boundaries are not weakness—they are wisdom.

Choosing humanity means:

- Logging off without apology
- Saying “not now” without fear
- Protecting personal time like oxygen

When you set boundaries, you are not falling behind.
You are **preserving yourself**.

Rest Is Not Laziness—It Is Resistance

Rest has become a radical act.

In a culture that worships hustle, resting feels like rebellion.
But even machines shut down for maintenance.

Humans need:

- Sleep to heal
- Silence to think
- Stillness to remember who they are

Choosing rest is choosing longevity over burnout.
Depth over exhaustion.
Life over survival.

Choosing Real Connection Over Constant Communication

We talk more than ever—and connect less than ever.

Messages have replaced conversations.
Reactions have replaced understanding.
Screens have replaced eyes.

Choosing humanity means:

- Looking at people, not phones

- Listening without planning replies
- Being present without multitasking

Connection is not about availability.
It is about **attention**.

Reflection: The Forgotten Human Skill

Machines process data.

Humans reflect.

Reflection is where growth happens.
Where lessons turn into wisdom.
Where noise turns into meaning.

Choosing humanity means asking:

- How am I really feeling?
- What am I becoming?
- Is this life aligned with my values?

Without reflection, progress becomes directionless.

Purpose: The One Thing Technology Cannot Give

AI can optimize your schedule.
It cannot tell you why you exist.

Purpose is what turns work into meaning.
Days into stories.
Effort into fulfillment.

Choosing humanity means:

- Doing things that matter, not just things that pay
- Measuring success beyond numbers
- Living with intention, not autopilot

Teaching the Next Generation What Matters

Children are watching us.

Not what we say—but how we live.

If we show them:

- Balance, they learn stability
- Empathy, they learn compassion
- Boundaries, they learn self-respect

The future is not coded in machines.
It is shaped by **what humans model**.

Choosing Humanity Is a Quiet Courage

You will not get applause for choosing rest.
You will not get awards for choosing presence.
You will not get recognition for choosing empathy.

But you will get something far greater:

- Peace
- Clarity
- Wholeness

And that is enough.

We Are Not Outdated

Technology will evolve.
AI will become smarter.
Machines will become faster.

But human emotions will never be obsolete.

Progress should upgrade life—not erase humanity.

Let us build a future where:

- Technology serves humans
- Work respects emotions
- Efficiency honors well-being

Because at the end of the day,
we don't want a smarter world
if it's a colder one.

The future is still human.

And it begins—with you.

The Choice That Defines Us

There will come a day when no one remembers how fast our machines were.

But they will remember
how tired people looked,
how disconnected families felt,
how silently humans struggled
in the most advanced era in history.

That day is not in the future.
It is already here.

And yet—this is not a chapter of fear.

It is a chapter of **choice**.

We Were Never Meant to Compete With Our Creations

Humans were not designed to win races against machines.

We were designed to **feel**,
to **connect**,
to **create meaning**,
to **carry stories**,
to **love deeply and imperfectly**.

The tragedy of this era is not that AI is becoming intelligent.
It is that humans are forgetting they already are.

When we compare ourselves to machines, we lose by default—

not because we are weaker,
but because we are measuring the wrong things.

The Silent Cost of Constant Optimization

We optimized productivity.
We optimized speed.
We optimized performance.

But we forgot to optimize:

- Rest
- Relationships
- Emotional safety
- Inner peace

We saved time—yet lost presence.
We gained efficiency—yet lost meaning.

This is not progress.
This is **disconnection disguised as success**.

What Machines Will Never Understand

A machine will never:

- Feel the weight of responsibility in silence
- Carry unspoken sacrifices for family
- Break internally and still show up
- Love without logic
- Choose kindness when it costs something

A machine will never understand what it means to be human—
because humanity is not an algorithm.

It is **experience**.

The World Does Not Need More Speed

It needs more understanding.
More patience.
More emotional intelligence.

It needs workplaces that see people, not just output.
Leaders who value well-being over burnout.
Families who protect connection over convenience.

The future will not be saved by smarter machines.
It will be saved by **wiser humans**.

Choosing Humanity Is an Act of Courage

It takes courage to slow down
in a world addicted to speed.

It takes courage to feel
in a culture that numbs.

It takes courage to say:
"I am human. I need rest. I need meaning. I need connection."

But courage has always been the foundation of change.

Conclusion

This Is Not the End—It Is a Beginning

If you reached this page,
you are not afraid of technology.

You are afraid of losing yourself inside it.

This book was never about rejecting AI.
It was about **remembering humanity**.

You are not outdated.
You are not replaceable.
You are not a resource.

You are a human being.

And that still matters—more than ever.

Let us move forward with technology in our hands
and humanity in our hearts.

Let us build a future where:

- Innovation respects emotion
- Work honors life
- Progress includes rest

Because the greatest intelligence
this world will ever know
is not artificial.

It is **human**.

And the future is still ours
—if we choose it.

ABOUT THE AUTHOR

Rakesh Singh is a thoughtful and emotionally driven author who writes about the unseen struggles, silent sacrifices, and inner lives of modern human beings. His writing gives voice to feelings people often carry but rarely express—especially men navigating responsibility, love, work, and identity in a fast-changing world.

He is the author of the widely appreciated books ***Under the Table*** and ***Man After Marriage***, both of which explore the emotional realities of life beyond appearances—where strength is quiet, pain is unspoken, and love is often misunderstood.

Rakesh completed his schooling at **Kendriya Vidyalaya, IIT Kharagpur (West Bengal)** and has a strong professional background in technology. He is a **Microsoft Certified AI Data Engineer**, **Microsoft Copilot Expert**, and **Python certified from IIT Madras**, with participation in multiple AI tool workshops conducted at **IIT Delhi**. His deep exposure to technology gives him a rare perspective—allowing him to write not just about machines, but about the humans living alongside them.

Despite working in advanced technology, writing has remained his passion since school days. He has won multiple writing competitions within and outside the organizations he has worked with. His stories are shaped by real experiences, real emotions, and real people.

Through his books, Rakesh highlights the emotional cost of modern life—how men silently balance family, marriage, work, and expectations, and how technology, progress, and pressure often ignore human limits. He believes that while technology can replace skills, it can never replace **emotions, empathy, or the human soul**.

Currently based in **Gurugram, Haryana**, Rakesh continues to write with one purpose:
to remind the world that behind every role, responsibility, and achievement, there is a human being who deserves understanding.

www.ingramcontent.com/pod-product-compliance
Ingram Content Group UK Ltd.
Pitfield, Milton Keynes, MK11 3LW, UK
UKHW041314190726
13845UKWH00025B/270